Soccerasaurus

by Robb Lawrence
illustrated by Tim Parker

ISBN 0-590-42312-6

12 11 10 9 8 7 6 5 4 3 2   2 3 4/9

Printed in the U.S.A.   10
First Scholastic printing, September 1989

SCHOLASTIC INC.

New York Toronto London Auckland Sydney

Watch out!

Soccerasaurus is going to kick another goal.

When he kicks the ball, it *knows* it's been kicked!

Every afternoon, Soccerasaurus played soccer in an empty lot with his friends.

They didn't have real goals or uniforms. And there were only five or six Saurus Gang kids — not enough for real teams.

But they didn't care. They always had fun.

Soccerasaurus gave the ball a powerful kick. The goalie tried to block it with his head. But the ball sailed right past him.

GOAL!

Soccerasaurus's side won the game.

"The only good thing about the end of a soccer game," said Soccerasaurus, "is that you get to start another one!"

Soccerasaurus and his friends started a new game. They ran back and forth, passing, kicking, and blocking.

Two dadasauruses came by and watched the game for a while.

"They shouldn't have to play soccer in this empty lot," said the first dadasaurus, shaking his head. "They don't have real goals with nets."

"They don't have any equipment at all," said the second dadasaurus. "Just a ball."

"And look how they're dressed!" The first dadasaurus frowned. "They don't have soccer uniforms."

"They don't even have the right number of players," both dadasauruses said at once.

Some other grown-ups came by. "We've got to do something about this," they agreed.

Even more grown-ups came. "But what should we do?" they asked.

"Let's start a soccer league for them," someone suggested.

"Great idea! They'll love it!" said a momasaurus.

"A soccer league. With uniforms, and real teams, and real goals with nets. They'll be so happy!" said a dadasaurus.

The grown-ups ran onto the lot and stopped the game. "Guess what, kids?" they announced. "We're going to start a soccer league for you."

"Oh. How nice," said Soccerasaurus and his friends.

The grown-ups fixed up a real soccer field.
And they bought uniforms for everyone.

Soccerasaurus and his friends tried on the
uniforms. They almost fit.

"What about the teams?" asked one dadasaurus. "My son should be on the Stars."

"My son should be on the Comets," said a momasaurus.

"My daughter should be captain of the Comets," said another dadasaurus.

"No. Your daughter should be on the Stars — not the Comets."

"Comets!"

"Stars!"

"But what about the Bluebirds? Who's going to be on the Bluebirds?" someone cried.

The grown-ups argued for a long time.
Finally the game began.

Soccerasaurus was happy. There was nothing
he liked better than a good soccer game. He
kicked the ball to a teammate. The teammate
kicked it back to him.

WHEEEEEET!

A referee blew his whistle. "Penalty!"
he cried.

"That was no penalty!" shouted a dadasaurus
watching the game.

The grown-ups argued again.

The game began once more.

WHEEET! The referee blew his whistle again. "Penalty!" he yelled.

The grown-ups all ran onto the field to fight about the penalty.

They fought and fought.

"I have an idea," Soccerasaurus told his friends.

First he had to get the grown-ups' attention. So he kicked the ball as hard as he could. It sailed across the field and into the net.

The grown-ups all turned around.

"You can settle your argument with a big soccer game," Soccerasaurus told them. He divided the grown-ups into two teams — the Stars and the Comets.

The grown-ups loved the idea. They ran out to play soccer.

They passed, and blocked, and kicked, and rolled on the ground, and played as hard as they could.

They forgot all about Soccerasaurus and his friends.

Soccerasaurus and his friends took off their uniforms. They went back to the empty lot.

Then they played soccer for the rest of the afternoon. Soccerasaurus scored three goals.

They didn't have uniforms. They didn't have real goals or equipment or referees. There were only four players to a team.

But they all had a wonderful time.

At the end of the game, the score was tied, six to six.

"The only good thing about the end of this soccer game," said Soccerasaurus, "is that we can start another one—*and* there are no grown-ups around!"